BOOKMARKS
AND
SCRIPTURE TOTES

**Counted Cross-stitch Designs
by Anne Lyon**

www.templehillbooks.com

ISBN 978-1-4341-0387-1

Contents

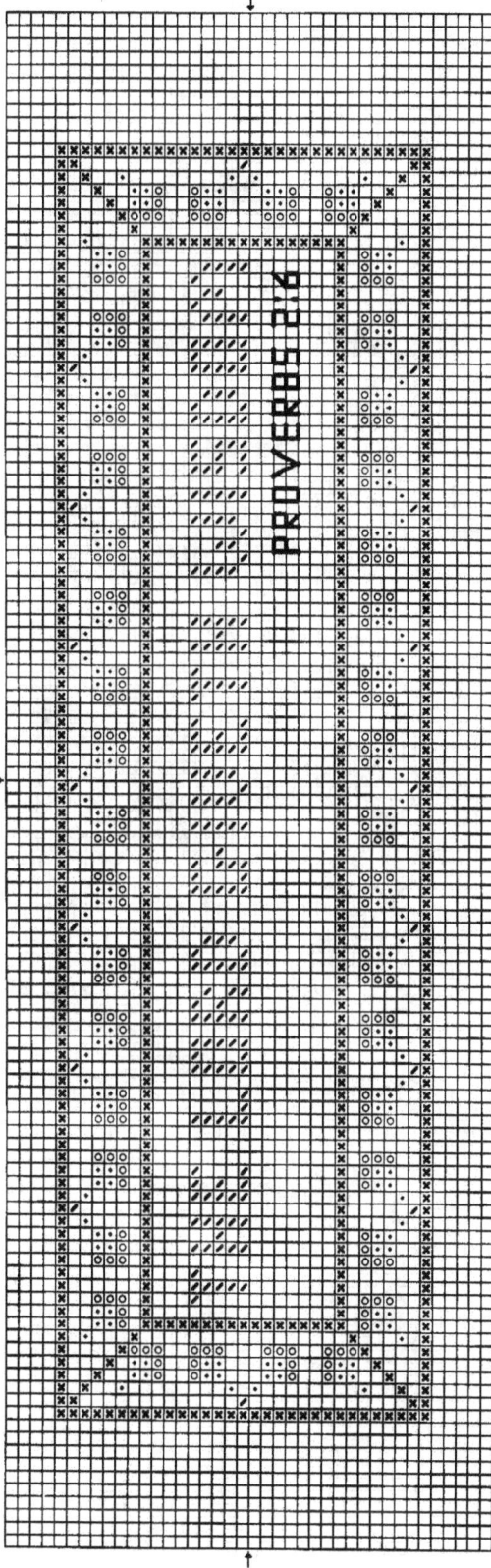

The Lord giveth wisdom.
Proverbs 2:6

black (DMC 310)
coral red, vy. dk. (DMC 817)
pearl grey, vy. lt. (DMC 762)
shell grey, dk. (DMC 451)
  Scripture ref: coral red, vy. dk. (DMC 817)

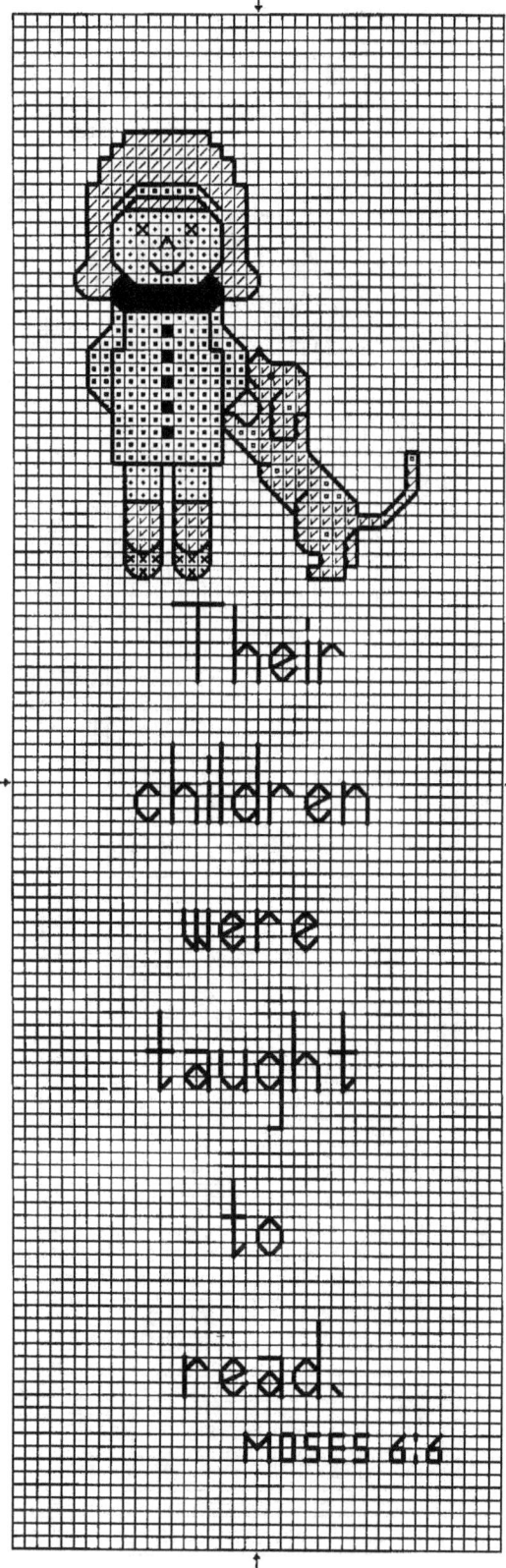

Their children were taught
to read. Moses 6:6

white (DMC white)   black (DMC 310)
coffee brown (DMC 838)
mohogany, dk. (DMC 400)
coral red, vy. dk. (DMC 817)
navy blue, dk. (DMC 823)
peach flesh, lt. (DMC 754)
  Girl's & dog's features: coffee br. (DMC 838)
  Lettering: navy blue, dk. (DMC 823)
  Outlining: black (DMC 310)

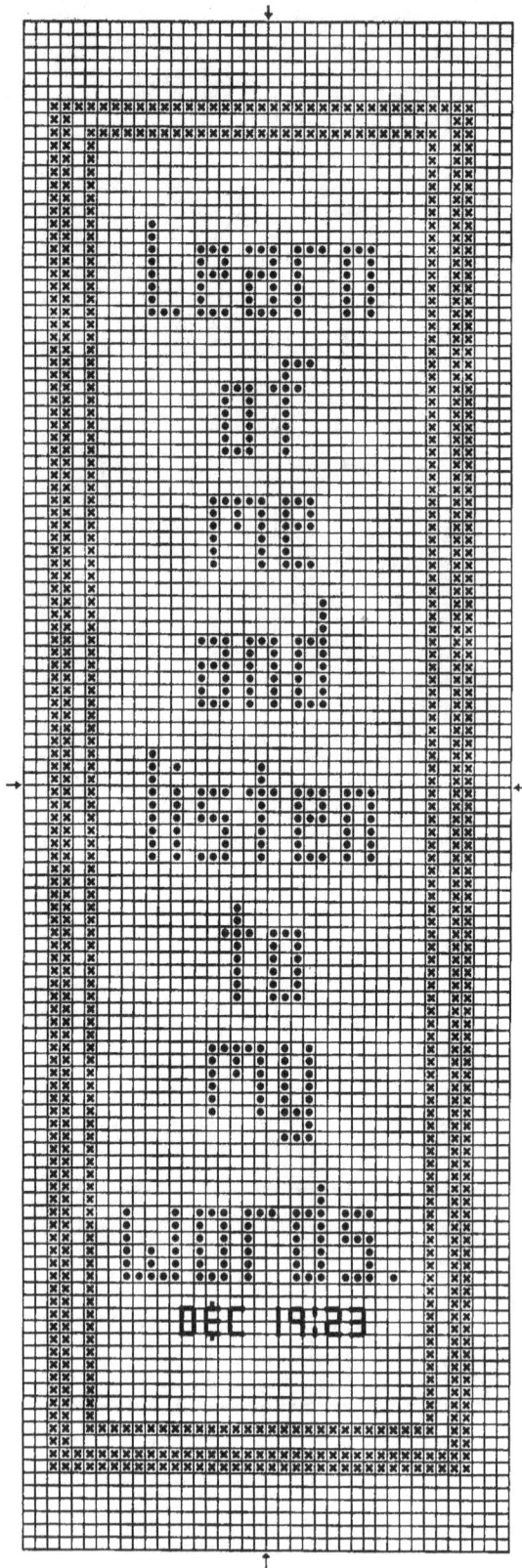

Learn of me and listen to my words. D&C 19:23

☒ blue, vy. lt. (DMC 827)
◉ navy blue, med. (DMC 311)
   Scripture ref: navy blue, med. (DMC 311)

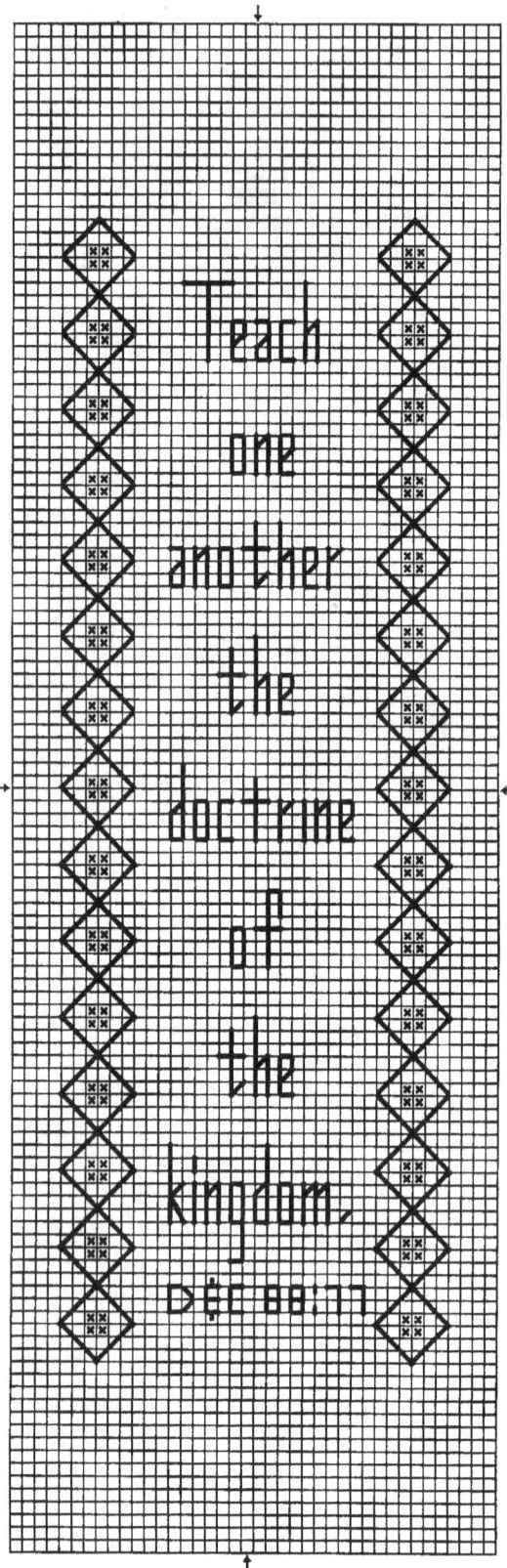

Teach one another the doctrine of the kingdom. D&C 88:77

◪ coffee brown (DMC 801)
☒ terra cotta, med. (DMC 356)
   Lettering: forest green, vy. dk. (DMC 986)
   Scripture ref: terra cotta, med. (DMC 356)

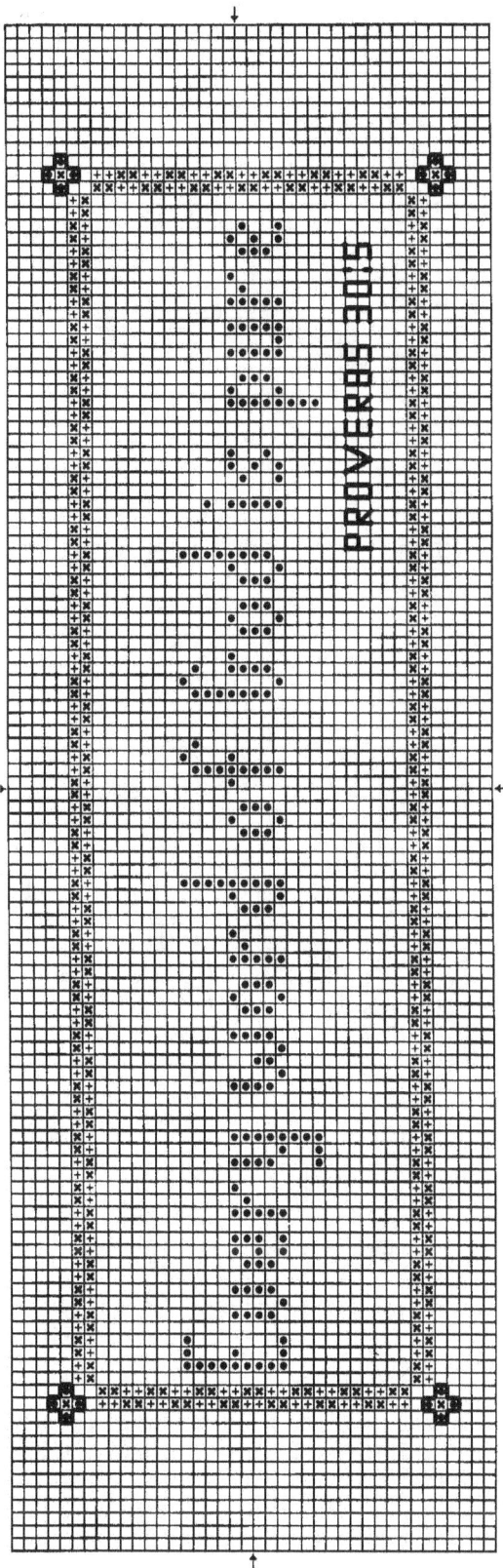

Every word of God is pure
Proverbs 30:5

☒pistachio green, lt. (DMC 368)
◉antique mauve, dk. (DMC 315)
⊞cornflower blue, lt. (DMC 794)
    Scripture ref: antique mauve, dk. (DMC 315)
    Outlining of corner flowers: cornflower blue,
    lt. (DMC 794)

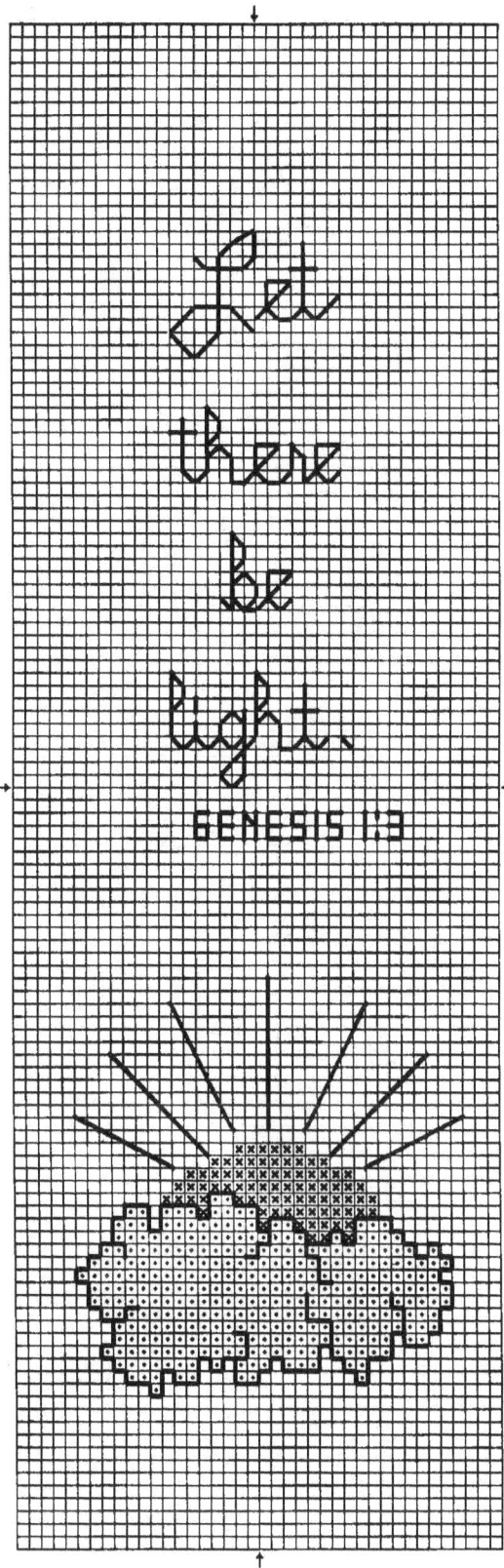

Let there be light.
Genesis 1:3

⊡white (DMC white)
☒yellow, pale (DMC 744)
    Sun rays: yellow, pale (DMC 744)
    Lettering: navy blue, dk. (DMC 823)
    Outlining: blue, lt. (DMC 813)

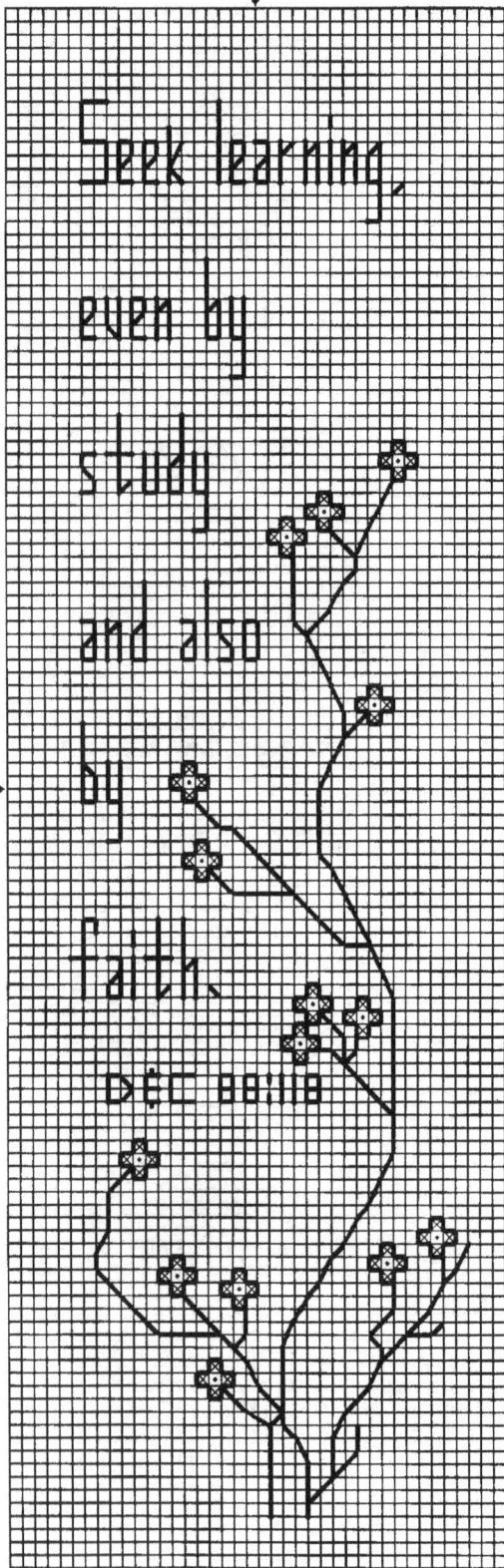

**Seek learning, even by study
and also by faith. D&C 88:118**

⊠shell pink, vy. lt. (DMC 225)
⊡drab brown, vy. dk. (DMC 611)
    Lettering: drab brown, vy. dk. (DMC 611)
    Outlining: rose (DMC 335)
    Flower stems: drab brown, vy. dk. (DMC 611)

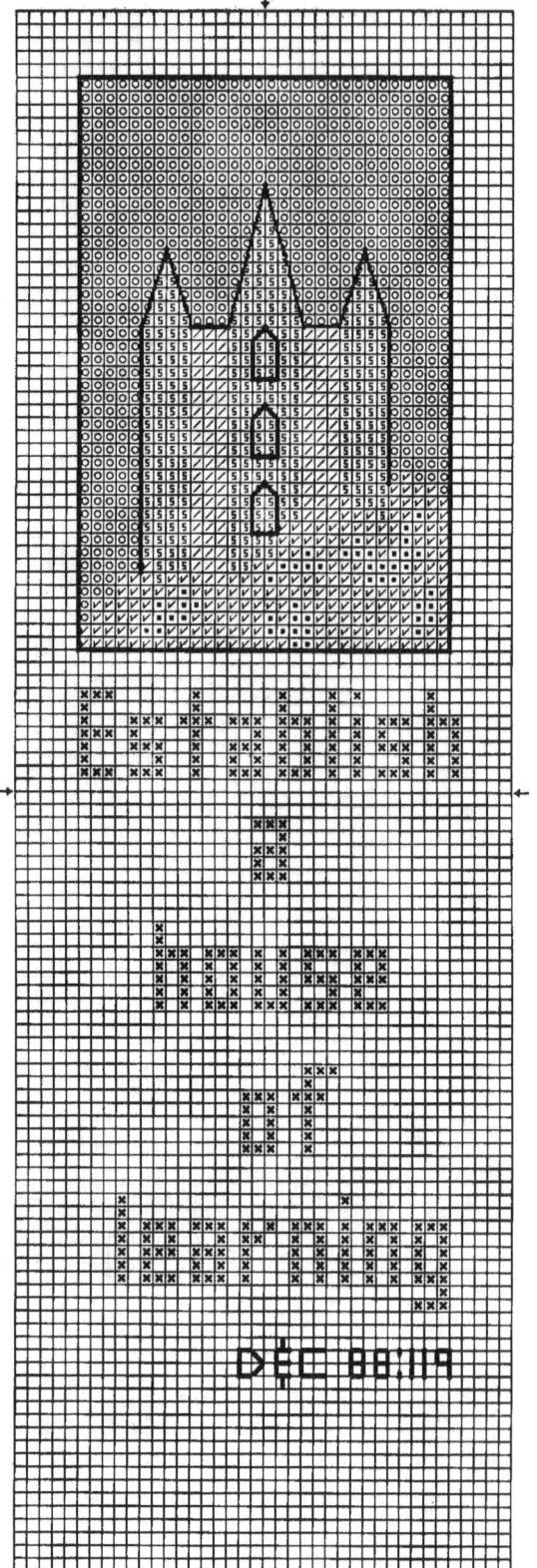

**Establish a house of learning.
D&C 88:119**

⑤steel grey, lt. (DMC 318)
⊠ash grey, vy. lt. (DMC 535)
⊿ash grey, vy. lt. (DMC 535)
⊿forest green (DMC 989)
▣forest green, vy. dk. (DMC 987)
⊙blue, vy. lt. (DMC 827)
    Scripture ref: ash grey, vy. lt. (DMC 535)
    Outlining: ash grey, vy. lt. (DMC 535)

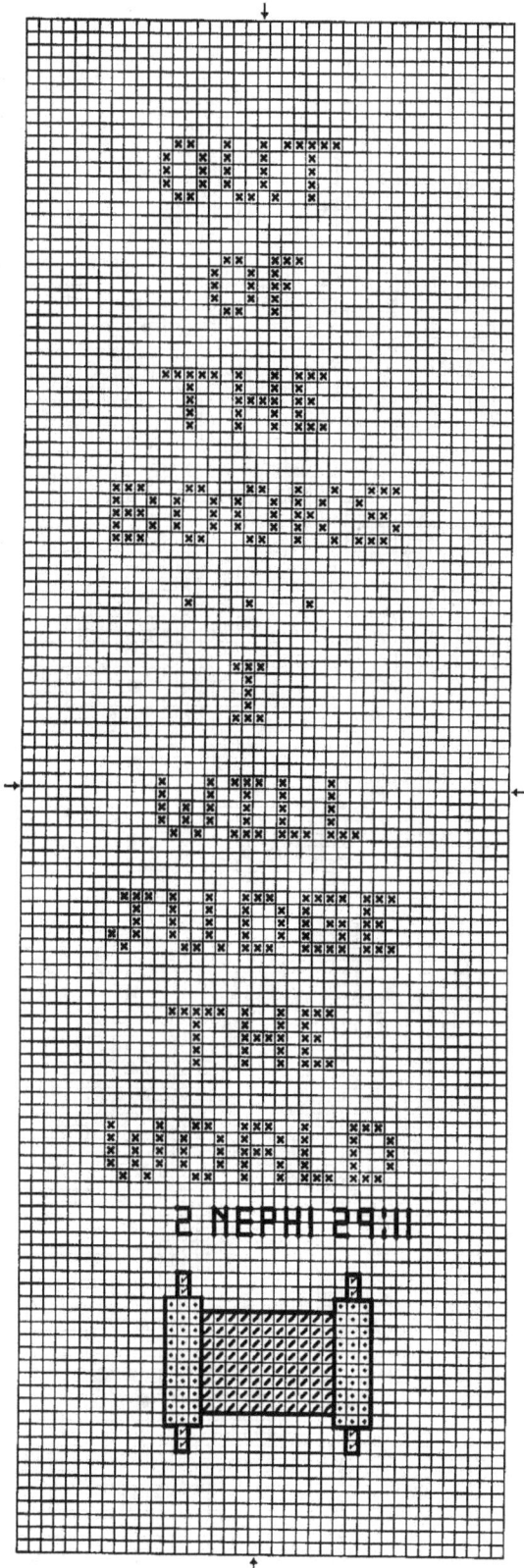

**Out of the books...I will judge
the world. 2 Nephi 29:11**

⊡ mocha brown, vy. lt. (DMC 3033)
⊠ tan, vy. lt. (DMC 738)
⊠ beige brown, vy.dk. (DMC 838)
☑ mohogany, dk. (DMC 400)
 Scripture ref: mahogany, dk. (DMC 400)
 Outlining: mahogany, dk. (DMC 400)

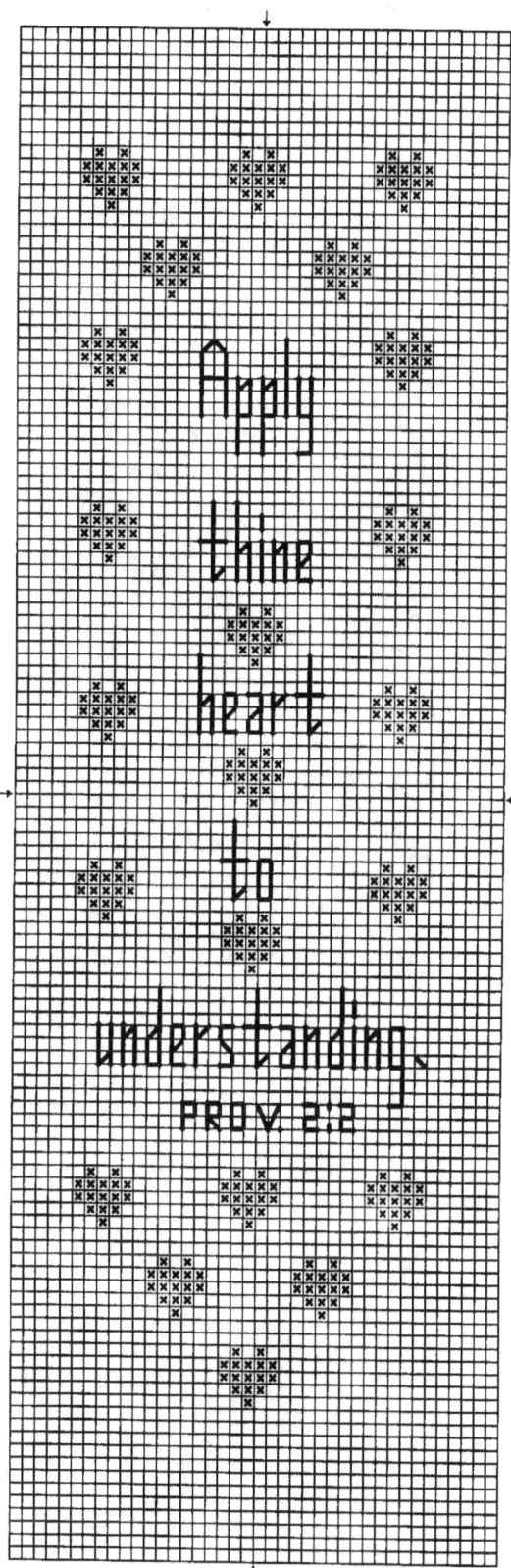

**Apply thine heart to under-
standing. Prov. 2:2**

⊠ rose (DMC 335)
 Lettering: navy blue, (DMC 823)

Happy is the man that findeth wisdom. Prov. 3:13

☒ antique mauve, med. (DMC 316)
⊡ Nile green (DMC 954)
▱ Nile green (DMC 954)
   Lettering: antique mauve, med. (DMC 316)
   Scripture ref: navy blue, dk. (DMC 823)
   Border: navy blue, dk. (DMC 823)

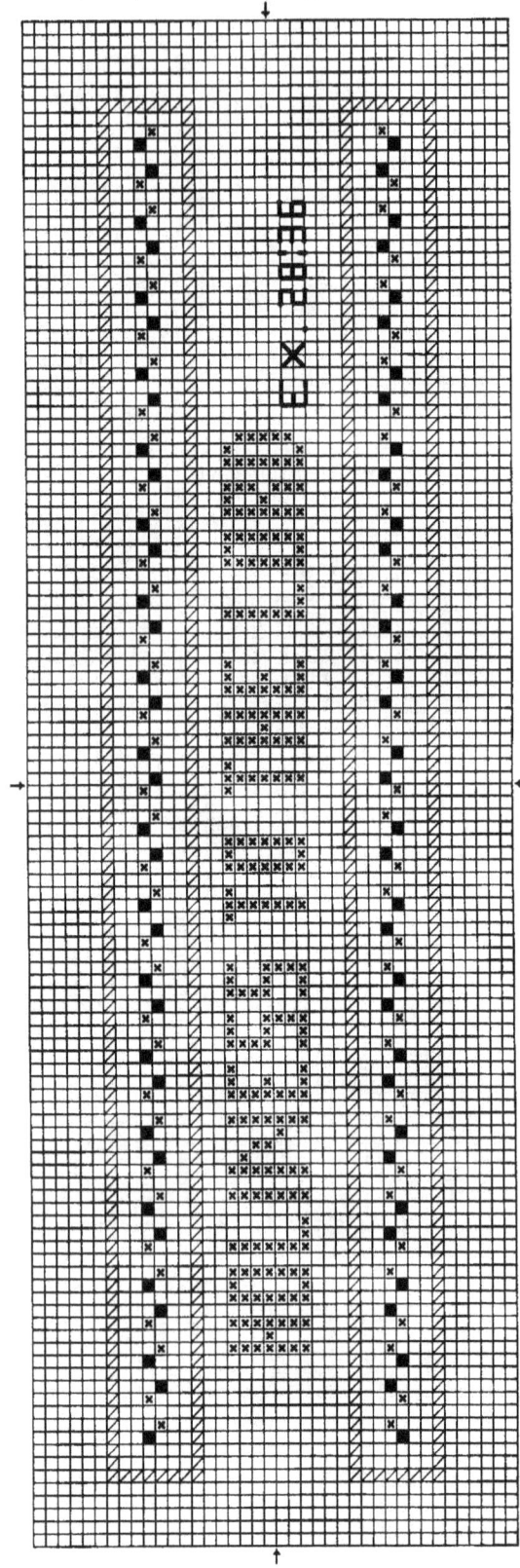

Holiness to the Lord. Ex. 28:36

▱ drab brown, dk. (DMC 611)
☒ black brown (DMC 3371)
◼ terra cotta, dk. (DMC 355)
   Scripture ref: drab brown, dk. (DMC 611)

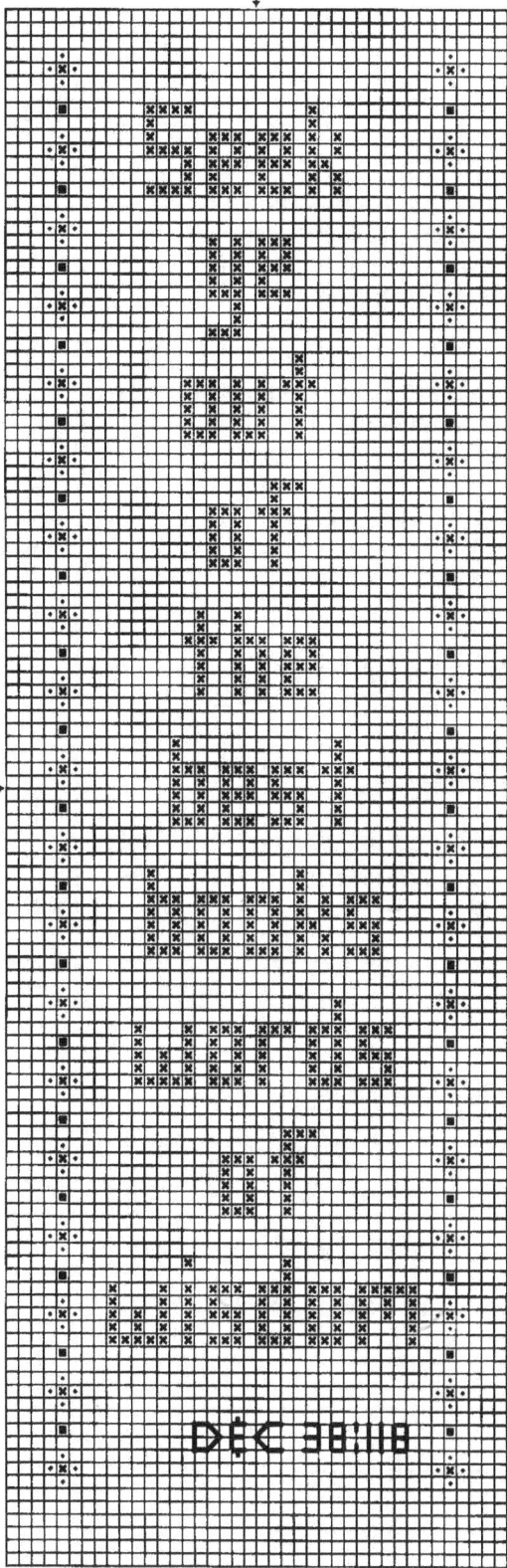

Seek ye out of the best books
words of wisdom. D&C 38:118

☒ salmon, med. (DMC 3328)
☐ blue green (DMC 502)
⊡ golden yellow, vy. lt. (DMC 3078)
   Scripture ref: salmon, med. (DMC 3328)

Assembling Bookmarks

You will need

1. Hardanger cloth (22 count) measuring 5 1/2" x 2".

2. DMC embroidery floss in the colors called for in the pattern or the color of your choice.

3. Grosgrain ribbon (1 1/2" wide by 8" long) in a color to coordinate with the DMC colors used in your cross-stitch.

4. Stitch witchery for fusing cross-stitch to ribbon.

Instructions

1. Find the center of the Hardanger cloth by folding it in half lengthwise and then in half widthwise. The center is the corner of both folds. Mark with a pin. You can begin in either of two ways: Start in the center and work out, or count up from the center of the cloth to where the pattern begins and start there.

2. Use one strand of the six-ply floss. Do not make a knot in the end. Pull the thread up through the cloth until about 1/2" is left on the underside. Catch this "tail" in your first few stitches.

3. When you are at the end of the floss, or changing colors, run your needle through a few stitches on the underside of your work and clip the thread. You should avoid making any knots.

4. When finished, gently wash in warm sudsy water. Do not scrub. Rinse. Place flat on a hand towel and roll up. Squeeze out excess water. Then place *face down* on a dry towel and press the back until it is dry.

Assembling Bookmark

1. Make a V-cut in both ends of the ribbon by folding it in half lengthwise. Make a diagonal cut beginning 3/4" down from the top on the *folded* edge and cutting up to corner edges of the ribbon.

2. Press ribbon and set aside.

3. Unravel each side of the bookmark by gently pulling four rows of threads from all edges of th cloth.

4. Place bookmark face down on a clean towel. Position stitch witchery over the bookmark so it meets the fringe on the bookmark but does not overlap it.

5. Center the ribbon over the bookmark and stitch witchery—be careful not to move stitch witchery.

6. Press for ten seconds. Do not press the front of your bookmark, only the back. Be careful not to scorch.

Assembling Scripture Totes

Materials needed

For regular-size scripture tote:
1. 1/3 yard double-sided quilted fabric (the single-sided fabric is not sturdy enough)

2. Small piece of medium-weight interfacing

3. 22-inch zipper in a color to match the fabric

4. 7 inches of 1-inch lace (optional)

5. 1 package piping in color to match tote (optional)

6. Matching thread

For large-print scripture tote:
1. 1/2 yard double-sided fabric

2. Small amount of medium-weight interfacing

3. 28-inch zipper (Coats and Clarks parka zipper)

4. 1 foot of lace (optional)

5. 1 package of piping in color to match tote (optional)

6. Matching thread

What to Cut

For regular-size scripture tote:
2 pieces—9" x 6 1/2" (front and back of tote) "A", "B"

2 pieces—7" x 3 3/4" (top) "C", "D"
1 piece—8 3/4" x 2 1/2" (handle) "E"
1 piece—6 1/2" x 5 1/2" (pocket) "F"
1 piece—4 1/2" x 22", then cut in half lengthwise
making 2 pieces measuring 2 1/4" x 22"
(boxing) "G", "H"
From medium-weight interfacing, cut 1 piece
8 3/4" x 2 1/2" for handle

For large-print scripture tote:
2 pieces—10 1/2" x 7 1/2" (front and back of
tote) "A", "B"
2 pieces—8 3/4" x 3 1/2" (top) "C", "D"
1 piece—10 1/4" x 2 1/2" (handle) "E"
1 piece—7 1/2" x 6" (pocket) "F"
1 piece —4" x 26", then cut in half lengthwise,
making 2 pieces—2" x 26" (boxing) "G", "H"
From medium-weight interfacing, cut one piece
4" x 26" for handle

Labeling Pieces

On eight small pieces of masking tape write the
letters "A" through "H" and tape each piece of
tape to its corresponding fabric piece.

Assembling Scripture Tote

*Note: All seam allowances
are 1/2".*

1. Inserting zipper (pieces
"G", "H")

a. If making the large-
print scripture tote,
measure 26" from the top
of the zipper and overcast
the zipper teeth several
times at that point to keep
the zipper from separating
at the bottom. Do not cut
off excess until zipper is
sewn in.

b. Fold under 1/2" on 1
lengthwise edge of "G".

c. Pin folded edge of
fabric to zipper, starting
1/2" from beginning of
zipper teeth and about
1/8" away from zipper
teeth the full length of
zipper.

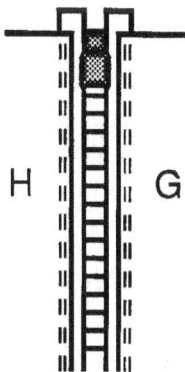

d. Using zipper foot, stitch close to folded edge
of fabric.

e. Sew a parallel line of stitching 1/4" away from
first line of stitching.

f. Repeat for left side.

g. For larger-size tote, cut off zipper 1" from
overcasting.

2. (Optional) Position cross-stitched piece on
front piece of fabric "A". Pin in place and stitch
around its perimeter just inside the fringed edge.

3. Pocket (pieces "A", "F")

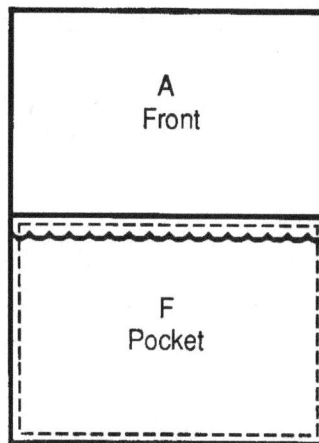

a. Decide which side of the fabric you want to
use for the pocket before doing the stitching.
Then fold down top longest edge of pocket ("F")
1/2" and stitch 1/4" from edge. Apply lace if
desired, sewing it over the top stitching on the
folded top edge. You may want to place a 1/4"
piece of ribbon or decorative machine stitch over
top edge of lace. If you are not using lace, fold
down top edge of pocket 1/4" and 1/4" again and
stitch close to edge.

b. Pin pocket to inside lower half of front piece
and stitch 1/4" from edges on both sides and
bottom.

4. Piping (Optional)

a. Machine baste around all four edges of both
front and back pieces, 1/2" from the edge.

b. Using a zipper foot, sew piping to right side
of each piece ("A", "B") lining up the stitching
on the piping with the basting on the front and
back pieces.

c. Clip the corners of the piping from the raw edge to the stitching so they will lie flat. Do not clip through piping. Do not clip the front and back pieces.

5. Boxing (pieces "A", "B", "G", "H")

a. Mark 1 3/4" in from top corners on long side of both "A" (front) and "B" (back).

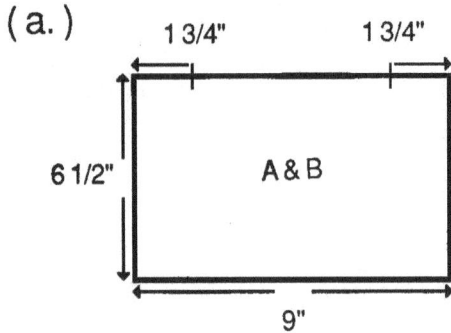

(a.)

1 3/4"   1 3/4"

6 1/2"   A & B

9"

b. Pin right side of "H" (boxing) to right side of "A" (front) beginning at and ending at marks.

c. Clip in 1/2" on boxing at the corners, so the boxing will lie flat. Do not clip the front and back pieces.

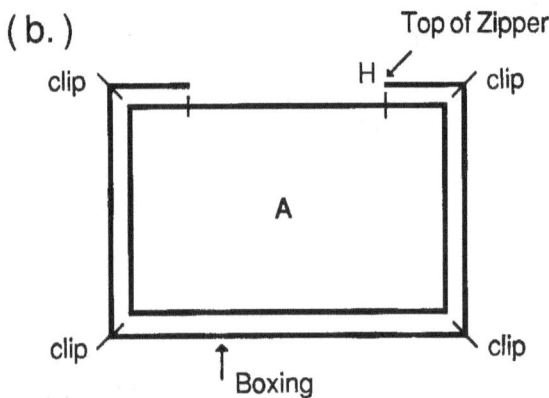

(b.)

Top of Zipper

clip   H   clip

A

Boxing

clip   clip

d. Machine stitch, beginning 1/2" from mark and ending 1/2" from mark on left side.

e. Repeat using "B" (back piece) and "G" (left side of boxing).

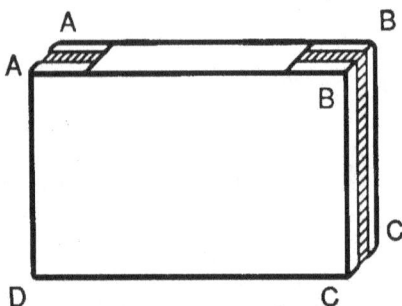

A   B
A   B
          C
D   C

f. All four corners on the front and all four corners on the back should be in alignment.

6. Top (pieces "C", "D")

a. Place right side of "C" and wrong side of "D" together. Stitch 1/2" seams on both short ends. Turn right side out. Now the right side of "C" and the wrong side of "D" will be facing out.

b. Unzip zipper and turn tote inside out.

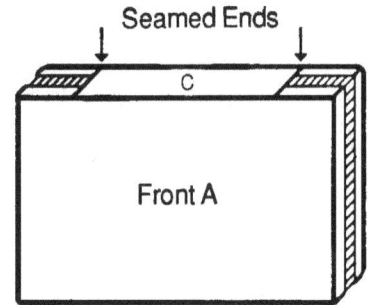

Seamed Ends

C

Front A

c. Pin piece between boxing and front side matching raw edges.

d. Stitch, overlapping stitching on main part of tote.

e. Repeat for back side.

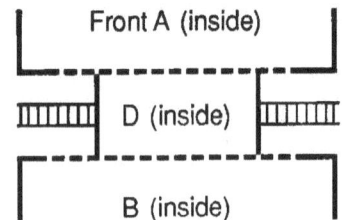

Front A (inside)

D (inside)

B (inside)

f. Turn right side out. The ends should be open at this time, so the handle can be fitted under in the next step.

7. Handle (piece "E" and interfacing)

a. Sew interfacing to wrong side of "E" (handle Stitch very close to edges.

b. Fold both long edges of handle under 1/4" and then entire handle in half lengthwise. Pin.

c. Top stitch through all layers 1/8" from edge both long sides of handle.

d. Place end of handle under 1/2" of unsewn top piece edge. Pin.

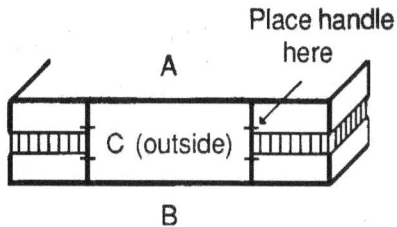

e. Top stitch across end of top piece ("C, D") through all thicknesses.

f. Fold handle back over top towards left side and tuck end of handle under "C" and "D" 1/2". Pin. Stitch 1/4" from edge across entire width of top piece. Stitch on top of previous stitching once or twice again to strengthen.

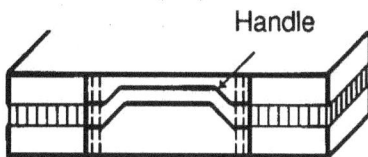

g. Repeat steps d, e, f for left side.

Note: This step could be sewn by hand if your sewing machine is not powerful enough to sew through all thicknesses.

8. Finishing

Trim inside seams to 1/4" and then zigzag close to edges.

www.ingramcontent.com/pod-product-compliance
Lightning Source LLC
Chambersburg PA
CBHW081238020426

42331CB00012B/3219

9 781434 103871